Yes yes yes! Bob Holman's poems explode with jounce and pounce!   —*Gwendolyn Brooks*

Bob's all the things and that's why I can't stop reading him or wanting to have lunch with him. He, the life poem, is silly, erotic, thoughtful, political before and after anyone, irrepressible and constant. How much can be like this and not be the very earth itself.   —*Eileen Myles*

This poetry on the tip of the poet's tongue. From his mouth to your ear. "Desperate to be a poet," he says, "desperate not to let anything escape. A young man whose father had killed himself when he was two, has found something that will never be lost . . ." And he gives this thing he has found to us, his grateful readers! This is the real thing!   —*Margaret Randall*

whimsical, this poem/saga of ice-cream and vinegar/drizzled with jest   —*Ali Cobby Eckermann*

In the life of the poet, life is the poem. Bob Holman has always worn his sleeve, openly, on his lucid heart; unfolding over his many loves; of language, of intimacy, of teaching, of wonder, of words. *Life Poem* is Holman's primal scream: all of us can be the poem!   —*Edwin Torres*

Bob Holman is the President of Poetry.   —*Andrei Codrescu*

When the definitive history of the downtown poetry scene is finally written, the name of Bob Holman will be central to the carnivalesque narrative of this most fluid of avant-gardes.
                              —*Michael Lindgren*

Up in embryo, spinning in pre landin' *gEar*. . .In the beginning . . .of BH's initial time a wholearth of *lines*, notes, full headed poems were bob bob bobbing along. With joy and flammable turnstyles, sound and anti-reason teased. . .Out of the blue. . . Ore reading treasure. . .Solid Bob. . .earthcode langue sign's. Decant'd d'cantor whine of the times. Wherever poemanations like these go to love.   —*Julie Patton*

Good job, Bob.   —*Lou Reed*

Half a century ago, in his twentieth year on this planet, Bob Holman set about to write a spontaneous book directly from his life. The result, a 100-page poem, *Life Poem*, does not remind me of any book that I've read. Instead it makes me think of Picasso's painting, *Les Demoiselles d'Avignon*, when the young painter, with an intuitive leap of intellect, painted a face, unrelated to the other Demoiselles, of an African mask upon one of them. So, *zut!* now I think of Holman as a Picasso-type artist. . . .To write a book-length at the age of twenty on no subject except himself has the *chutzpah* and the energy that we expect from Picasso. And there is always a war beneath the outer surface. In *Life Poem*, it is Vietnam. Picasso and/or Holman or Holman and/or Picasso, best fits my understanding of this book by the 20-year old poet. It is no ordinary book but a treasure, spontaneous from the heart. Treasure it!! Holman and the Demoiselles of Avignon. The Demoiselles and Bob Holman. Treasure it!!

—*Michael McClure*

Bob Holman has two books coming out, written fifty years apart! Well, we're up to something then.

Even fewer years apart, Bob knew how to surprise and amaze me.

In 1996, he put me between two ladies in pink, to open the Annual Grand Slam at the Nuyorican Poets Cafe.

In 2003, we jammed with South African musicians near the Kruger National Park.

In 2011, Bob caught me totally unexpectedly in Addis Ababa.

In 2019, he'll have me stay in his guest room, holy grounds where so many famous poets slept.

I'm already looking forward to 2026!   —*Jaap Blonk*

Bob Holman reaches into the past to come up with a poem completely current and simultaneously eternal in its political and social implications. The year was 1969, and seemingly, little has changed. We've just gotten older. Despite the dire state of the country/world/universe, something deeper is happening, and ultimately – as Jack Kerouac said Charlie Parker's music said – all is well.   —*Vincent Katz*

LIFE POEM

Bob Holman

YBK Publishers

New York

Life Poem

YBK Publishers, Inc.   Bowery Books
39 Crosby Street   308 Bowery
New York, NY 10013   New York, NY
www.ybkpublishers.com   www. bowerypoetry.com

ISBN:978-1-936411-54-2

Library of Congress Catalog Card Number 2019948590

Manufactured in the United States of America for distribution in
North and South America or in the United Kingdom or Australia
when distributed elsewhere.

For more information, visit www.ybkpublishers.com

Cover design by Mike Tully

Original design by E. R. Pulgar

Front cover photograph and hand coloring © by Catherine Kucharski
Zinkevich at Cummington Community of the Arts in 1969, renewed 2019

Back cover photograph © Ariel Clute, 2019

Foreword

Life Poem is a young man's love poem to poetry. At age 21, I was completely filled with New York as poem with Kenneth Koch as my primary guide, Donald Lev as my interlocutor to the scene, and the Beats and the New York School as immediate kin. The summer I spent at the Cummington Community of the Arts in 1969 was a full-scale kidnapping and I was granted a living art heart ransom. This was the year Cummington switched from being a school with teachers, students, and curriculum into a self-structuring community where everybody was everything, aka, the '60s.

James Baker Hall based his novel *Music on A Broken Piano* on the place. Tar Lee Sun was an emissary from Sun Ra whose moaning and scatsongs filled our dormitory barn with the music of the spheres, worlds populated solely by poets, artists, and musicians. Suddenly everything was poetry, every observation, every dish to be washed, every memory, every drug-induced spaceshot into consciousness, all three moons. The flag pole I cut down in the woods that clonked me on the skull. My play, in which the entire population of Cummington was cast, so we were all both the players and the audience, was called *The Complete History of the Universe from the Beginning Till Now*. It was a big hit and came in under half an hour. I wish I could find it.

But I *was* able to find *Life Poem*. A cross between Pound and cummings and Koch, with a lot of Berryman, Stein, Yeats, Ginsberg, Baraka, O'Hara, French Surrealists, Chinese T'ang poets. A dash of Lorca, who had lived across the hall at John Jay at Columbia, some David Henderson as *De Mayor of Harlem*, Victor Hernandez Cruz's *Snaps*—

you get the picture. Kenneth Ketchum lent me his copy of Ted Berrigan's *Many Happy Returns* and here were Chris Horton, Elizabeth McKim, John Champoux, Kenneth Ketchum, Chuck Malzenski, Richie Silberg, Peter Zummo, Stephanie Woodard, Carol Wincenc, Nora Ryerson, Nancy Meader, Summer Lewis, Meredith Briggs, Joe Bernard, so many other Cummington co-artists. Let's go visit Richard Wilbur who lived just over the hill on the William Cullen Bryant estate. Paul Zinkievich, the wonderful artist who did the cover for the accompanying volume to this book, *The Unspoken*, was my trip buddy. And his girlfriend now wife of 40 years Catherine Kucharski took the photo of me on this cover, and did the coloring, too—coloring black and white photos was her job at the time.

"Desperate now I've started to write down everything that comes into my head" it starts, and I was desperate. Desperate to be a poet, desperate not to let anything escape. A young man whose father had killed himself when he was two years old finds something that will never be lost, be forever accepting and loving. Life fits into poem the way that *meaning is nested in sound,* as Walter Ong says. It moves on the flicker of your eyelash, the flicks being 24 frames per second, the movie we're watching/living transcribed as poem. The poem that is always being spoken. You just have to catch it, the way Dolphy catches music on *Last Date,* except that once you've heard it, it isn't gone. It's become the poem, and lives on.

Bob Holman

July, 2019

March 10, 1971

Hello.

Enclosed is a submission for the 1971
United States Award. This is a book-
length poem, called Life Poem.

There is a slight problem I have noticed
here. I'm currently living in New York.
This address is written on every page.
But I really doubt I'll be here come
fall-hope not. So the SSE has my
parent's address, and any correspondence
after June should be sent to them.
No chance of their leaving Cincinnati
nossir.

So here it is and I'm going to miss it.
Hope you have as much fun reading it as
I did in the writing part.

Robert Holman

Through June
3117 Broadway
Apt 37
NY NY 10027

After June
7000 Gammwell Dr
Cincinnati, Ohio

FROM ME AND MINE
TO YOU AND YOURS

Autobiography
Life's a funny place to be.
—Bob Brown, *1450–1950*

the clam
sits
ruminates spits
devours evolves

my head the percolator
my songs the queer brew

desperate now, i've started to write everything that comes
  into my head
i just lay it out right here
as if the lined paper had become some sort of garbage
  disposal
accepting and grinding everything i can throw out
if this were a giant baseball game, this paper would be
        Willie Say Hey Mays, great center-fielder, making
            deliciously slow
        basket catches of every ball hit by every batter
        in either league

somebody asked me today why i wasn't writing more.
i told them my muse is on vacation to the Riviera to get
  some sun.
'oh,' they said, 'i hope she enjoys it.' 'She will,'
i said 'except she has no breasts so her bikini doesn't work
unless the wind is blowing from behind her, so that the cups
blossom out like little butter cups—

meanwhile the Uruguay revolution
occupies this section
it is of Luis Cordoles
the 'George Washington of his Country'
and people shout—'save us, Luis'
and Luis, he ride on his big horse
and gets the town!
all the children yell & cheer at Luis—'Hey! Great! Atta boy!'
and Luis just rides off
he's very satisfied at night, being the GW of his C

ooh—i see ghosts
i call up the dead!
oh!

who is it but some leukemia victim
gasping right beside me—oh!
some white tight grip blooded thing
she is choked with fear
and she is choked with blood
not very good blood, this blood has
strange cells and these cells
commit willful murder on themselves

'there's a certain throbbing, i mean i can't explain it.
a sort of steady death pain, i dunno, i get poetical
about it and really i just want to get rid of it, it's
worst when my eyes bleed.'
'does that happen often?'
'only when the lids make quick contact.'
'you mean like a blink? you mean your eyes bleed every
    time you *blink?*'
'yeah. groovy, huh?'

around this place is a thin strip of Austria
the green central figure of the barren plains
that led us to the Great War—yes, the first
is always the best
and some little Hungarian peasant runs screaming, holding
    his penis
blood and intestines leaving a filth path behind him
he yells 'i die for you! i die for you!'
then he does

to wash, the Ibos
ram their clothes through
small holes in wicker baskets which
scrape the dirt off
occasionally a washerwoman
will be so lucky
as to discover
a left-over pearl

Om Mani Padhme Hum
i smell the blood of an Englishmun
sit beside me, lie beside me
Amen, the thunderbolt
Amen, the Dark Void
Amen, you and holy
Amen, me and holy

why do we play such games
can't we realize our bodies
somebody once taught me to wash behind my ears
now, years later, i have washed layer after layer of dirt and
    skin
from behind my ears
soon i will hit the bone
that's good—then i will not have to wash—i can polish …
but sex is different
and our bodies become intrinsically offal things
oh! to hold you is so sweet, yet you resist
not even the wild tongs of bath oil and spray deoderants
make me less the dirty thing

i confess, i think of your vagina
and your little hair hump
and today i shall slick down my old hair
and wear a suit of morning sun
visit you with daisy arm
and finally take you to bed
'i know your mother never taught you these things'
i will whisper, and then—off with my morning sun suit
and with only our body toys
commence to love on the quilt that took your grandmother
12 years to sew

the fortune teller insisted i had a baby
i smiled & said, 'i don't know of any.'
o! what if there is this little baby somewhere
and his mother feeds him through her body...
i knew that girl, yes i did
and i left her
now her mother is a grandmother, and she yells at the boy
    child,
'Don't grow up and be like your father, the bum!' ...
i sit here looking at a grass field & feeling the wind
not knowing i even have a baby
somewhere is my baby, looking over a dirty back lot
not even knowing he has a father who loves him very much

and me, well,
i'm the last frantic butterfly of the grass waves
and holiness of me is encompassed only by
the space about me, which
is in turn encompassed by others, eventually
and ultimately you, you of the shy smile

and if i keep on truckin' long enough
i'll just truck all my blues away

*   ***   *

the image here is that of
a giant hang-nail
a certain man on the dangling section
connected to the corpus by only a blade of hard and horny
  dead skin
filed at and dug at
he resists, causing pain to the main body
his is the death wish of a gaunt society,
the talons of a krawking magpie
the very finger that guides this pen
can guide a howitzer 40.5
at a crowd of starving enemies

how do you tell your son of wars?
my father never talked about it at all,
though i know now he was a sort of
semi-hero at the Battle of the Bulge, a
major general (one star) in the Checkerboard Division
he crossed the Remagen Bridgehead and won at
least a Purple Heart and Silver Star
he no longer keeps a lugar on the table
by his great master bed, oily thing
he won't go hunting, either...
sometimes i see him as hardened and leather tough,
sharpening his razor on his face,
a uniform on him. he controls men.
my father, one star, one man, will lead
the old 99th out time and again on missions
the ghosts of the men lost form gray swirls
in his breath on a cold day

thrash!
through my own head
the dull red cymbal music
collaborating with my own heart
and the mysteries rattle back and forth
my own body the sea
the waves forming songs of blood ovals
curling through the rays of my body

i live!
the thunder of my smile!

ever and always, Paris morning
and the mustached owner of
the Église Cheese Store
pushes the bolt to the side
turns on the light and sighs
cheese! the world, and Mme. Boncour arrives
she needs the Paris morning paper
and gradually, in carefully clocked syncopation
the Paris morning pushes the city
and with imperceptible calm and detachment
shakes her tousled Paris morning head

meanwhile, i feel that politics
has been bypassed for other games
so i suggest (as ever) anarchy for lovers
and for the pale-face, a constant revolution
a coup d-état a year, orders the Great Political Doctor
and no longer will you worry over boredom
and also—sales of newspapers will rise
and also—little children will know history

think!
may my words meander over you?
and what if you would like to push alongside?
greetings! i cry—for this is
the world's largest bowl
of alphabet soup
and as many cooks as necessary
and the necessities are infinite
and on the outside of us – the melting pot
and on our inside—the spices of joy

again does she speak the soft words
what will love mean today?
like some alien moth i try time and again
to unite with the soft glow
again and again repulsed by the heat

what if i laughed louder?
could you believe me then?

automobiles take over!
a cacophony of tuba horns
as the mainstay becomes oil and gasoline
and lubricants, thick grease, replace soap
cars, decide our economy!
Marx would love you, ah!
in your power is the bourgoisie—the
Plymouths and the Buicks! take them to *work*,
let them feel in their fingers
the blisters of communal life!
autos! drive them to the needed places!
hallelujah! car tv's, car tv dinners, car deoderants!

now is Joanie singing and seeing
she is blind and i say, 'Joanie,
the world is a poem.' and she says
in a voice quiet as some patterned princess,
'your eyes must be very soft'
o God, that she can feel my tears

today again the helicopter buzzed me
i often think it's papa, up from Florida
his new gadget under his masonic hand
'here,' says the helicopter 'am i, piloted
by a 70-year-old Jew who once sold
pots and pans door-to-door in Harlan.
now he flies me all the way up to the
wilds of Massachusetts just to say hello to his grandson'
and my zaydeh, my papa, will lean his cranky tired lean
out the window of the army surplus helicopter
and he will shout, 'Robbie, Robbie! Lookit what
i'fe got! a new eevenshun—and a new wife too,
Robbie, a new Bubbeh—
Robbie, she looks just like a movie star!'

fly away, fly away
the day birds will roost
fly in sight, come in sight
the night birds will arise
and the cycles of birds
meetings only at the time clock twice a day
and owls of course never make it with the robins

        *   ***   *

my life style came into question again today
all i could do was sort of laugh nervously
and high-tail it off to my buddies
i should've said—'i live for the moment, yet
i am a Christian in actions & have studied Buddhism &
    Christian Science,
and i am of the religion of man!'
i'll say it now for whatever good it does,
and though it isn't a complete statement,
it purges as well as any

the romantic apple of Eve fame
was offered to a young lad of 12 yesterday
by his maiden aunt of around 40
she was so lonely and while baby-sitting
in her nightgown (so hot) and she urged him to
and very scared oked the new game
nervous her hands twisted the zipper and it
broke through her stick fingers and her blood
gushed in symbols on the grass-stained pants

there is a slight wind now
and the Chief senses the storm so
calls his wise men around him to
speak of his age, and his hopes for
his oldest son, still a sapling (how long
he had waited to father a son!)
the storm came and the elders huddle together
to protect the Chief from his predicted fate
ah! the sun! the Chief lives!
ah! dark death on the plains,
the heir trampled by horses stampeding to
escape the effects of the rain

the passageway lights as brilliant as always
she leads the young couple, just married
to the nice room on the second floor
guests! always good to have guests!
a little money, a little company
oh! says the young girl, it's lovely!
twinkling at the fairy room, canopied bed
sea through the windows, hardwood floors
i'm sure you'll like it, as was always said
she left them then, and they fell to laughing on the
big cube bed, and its canopy became a tunnel leading to
clustered star nests, seen as they made very soft love

the old man went shopping and got a ride back
a week's work of food for him and the missus
and a ride back that leaves him on the
wrong side with two filled up grocery bags
and a parade mile of cars gives him no space to cross to
   home
and the missus watches her tired old man, ten years retired
struggle as the cans of vegetables tear through
the bags and dent as they fall like heavy rain to the
   pavement

university students of the world, ignite!
burn yourselves from both ends—
& the part left in the middle—that's you!
i hear so many people say 'i'm being used'—& they are!
so, a simple suggestion—use yourself! move around, polka!
there's nothing like a good polka to set yourself straight—
and tweedle clarinet ooompah accordian polkas are about
   all this
civilization has to offer

i am too far away not to touch you
this rain makes me laugh—in the morning and i laugh
because it comes fast but doesn't get me wet, just tickles
   me
course it makes my sweater fuzzy, beard too
you're too far away, coming in disguises, i'm forever
   touching you

my mother is a great one for toothpaste
every time she visits me, she brings a little package
of cookies and fruits and the inevitable Crest or Pepsodent
and packages from home, too—always the white tube …
my third drawer (personal effects) is being gradually filled
with them, even though i brush my teeth fairly often
i can see me now on my honeymoon
opening up my samsonite suitcase
revealing 30 tubes of assorted pastes

a reminder—someone just died in Viet Nam
a human
inter all these words with him, i loved him
i cry a gutter full of wasted widow's tears

we just don't give sagas a chance today
imagine Stephen Vincent Benet, waiting
for the newspapers of today's sagas:
'Politician has Auto Accident & Leaves Dead Blonde'
'We're Killing 10 Times As Many Of Them As They Are Of
    US'
'Awful Things Done To People'
headlines like these make horrible rhymed couplets

this is the inevitable cynicism of being hungry
having your lady be away
and doubting your own self:
you lash out at everything around you
hoping for your eyes back

there are grapes on a table in this room
they are a present from this person
who didn't know we should boycott grapes
for every grape bought a campesino starves!
there is a plastic tent over these green seedless grapes
like a shroud

when in Sweden
eat the special Swedish dish puchasable at many hot dog
    stands near
the university:
it is a big pliable round piece of bread, similar to a tortilla,
        formed into a cone, filled with mashed potato gobs
            and one
        long hot dog
this is very filling, one a day is best, plus an apple
and if you don't like it—give it to a passing hungry person
she will say 'Tak,' if Swedish or Danish
or—you can throw it into the sea and watch the seals fight
    over it,
        mashed potatoes being a great delicacy among seals

              *   ***   *

here in the cold land, the land of my brother
i sit wrapped in my love, her finger tendrils lip my mouth
sitting, calling out the sun over these 40 people of our life
no one had noticed the cricket by the fireplace
and that the sun (NOW) peers in had caused no stir
my love and i, surrounded by the 40
gutted and covered by their loneliness

how does man communicate
and more, why?
do these words come up from my soul, my ego
and where is the artist in me hiding and sniffling?
we are as entrenched as corpses in the grave
rationalized earth

'should we got to the garden?'
'i dunno ... ok, i guess.'
'have you been there before?'
'yeah, but it was a while ago.'
'i'm sorry—we don't have to go ...'
'IT'S OK LET'S GO TO THE GARDEN'

somewhere above us, some miles
a strange point, a halo, the pyramid apex's echo
and thwacking down—giant feet!
smooth, smooth with blisters, the long journey
no music, yet rhythmic silence
treading down, the huge heel and tank toes
hard heavy steps that leave no imprint
trudging that journey to earth
there, level out settle down, never-to move
there to form the calloused continents
there to be walked upon

cigarette stains so deep on his fingers
and a tormented head that shakes out a smile
Ken, the innocent reviled, is a strange calculator
not ever evil, calculating the sneaky path, incantations
he sits, forever non-believing, the blonde rock flowed
    around
rubber Ken, the calculator, the poet's vast warehouse

ho ho! laugh out a dream!
and a close one, that one
almost had me fooled!

in San Juan sits a woman
painting her fingernails red
painting hands and painting her wrists
burping and singing the alcohol sting
cover her elbow her shoulder her breast
AND—cover the belly the legs the feet
ah, the slick red paint!
nestle the paint jar into the crack
let flow the paint up through her body
red red, the woman is red
dead dead the baby is dead

why, when this 35-year old man talks to my friend
does it always sound like a lecture?
that the aged one will be wise
and the younger acquiesce to this wisdom
i'll yell at them—hey! guys—don't call for a vote
don't lecture, don't listen
let's call out the jingle bell parade people
and declare today, this day of words—Christmas!
point your toes—symbolically!

my Grendl, my sea-hag
my ruby-throated sea weed love!
if you kiss me will i kiss you?
well, me arm's harm run

mail for me?
just a little note takes me back
—man, product of his memories
   always reaching back, pulling dragging full
   thrusting out before him all the thoughts of before
   and hand over hand towards tomorrow

a sigh, the old Dutchman leans over the canal
his only son is a man now, married
ready to occupy the green chair
ready to sell tulip bulbs to the world
Philomon, the old man's wife, older still, remarkably
   vibrant
all these people must now take care of him
age, and the once provider now to be provided for
the Dutchman speaks soft gutteral words to the canal:
'that was my life, you see, now i'm a sore, to be cared for'
and the canal answers:
'i need you, your body will add to my vital chemicals.
my chemicals feed the flowers that flower the world.'
the old Dutchman, Norman, splashes, is covered
plants himself with worn hands, blossoming

the exotic in the familiar
the piranha
we sit next to a fog black lake
she whispers cunning words to me
kissing, never to come up for air
making love like the fireflies, the fish lure
she is laughing
i am being eaten alive in tiny bites

what? all my friends married?
and at one wedding? lined
up in pairs, each blessed, each now in blissful harmony—
ah! what a ceremony! such pomp!
the music of my musician friends
the crying of my nostalgic friends
the chuckles of my ironic friends
the Great Marriage, and the Great Marriage Feast
my girl friends, given away
my male friends, taken off
and here, my love and i sit writing presents, and laughing
and occasionally exchanging our love looks
for sizings-up

Lillie, the late, the soldier's solace
arises of the mossy entrance
twisting the ragged print dress
the walking shroud
the pie-faced private's fantasy
soul dream of the last bombed survivor
Lillie, the lady, sexy ghost child
walks again, the final premonition

to speak blah of heart gone
          'i really can't understand it
          she never really asked for anything,
          just smiled a lot, you, know?
          then leaves cause of no reason
          god, i can't understand women at all.
          if only she'd told me what i was doin' wrong.'
which was nothing really
just the wrong ball in the wrong pocket

praise now the germy microscopes
the silent no-world that clashes
with the white silk
this dainty miss sacrifices her nose
this elegant man gives up his kneecap
a sufficient struggle inside each of us
and slowly, but momentarily, all giving up the ghost

she had stacked the fifty-two before me
refused to allow a cut
and dealt from the bottom
i played deftly in gloves
blindfolded under my armor suit
fooling her,
slipping my naked big toe into her vagina

his tribe around him, Magic Manny, the tender beard
the true mind-poet allows no reality
he stands, smiles, seeks to guide
his plow plods Marx, and scoots about nature
he's a giant soft heart with a mission!
the tribe seeks place; firmly, he allows no place
his intellect, most gentle of the iconoclasts,
even in the innermost reality, defines
and, in which, violent blind light, causes certain
    destruction

past me on the highway flies
the Consolidated Cigar Corporation olive-green bus
laughing inside are the jostled tobacco strippers
on their way back to dinner
ho ho ho ! the laugh riots
ho! there is murder in the air
the driver strangled with ripping hemp
cigars stuffed in his nose and 5 in his mouth
now young Vincent takes the wheel, flips secret switch
the birth wings unfold, prop whirls
ho ho ho, boys!
and ease up on the stick, Vincent, there's a long way to go

salt crystals in his beard
eyes frozen to the bow
it is ABS, the old sea dog
hobbling about on wood leg, the archetype
storied of storms and women
he's done it all, seen the world
once he even saw a gold staircase leading to the stars
and he wasn't even drunk!
he keeps looking for it now,
the old salt, practicing up to steer the ketch
straight up the stairs

the haze covers the projectile
the haze covers the feathered gunner
in the city it is light

the first breath, victory
the lone fat man climbs aboard
the abandoned vessel
he is contracted, eyes to knees, vanishing penis mouth foot
the jumble ball of a man
unzipped and skeleton removed
a lymph gland
puddle

the superstition has arrived!
the thirteenth broken mirror and the little boy!
    'can you diagnose it?'
    'well, there's a regular swelling and receding'
    'yes, but what's wrong with him?'
    'there's a constant movement inside—ALRIGHT—
        i think he's ALIVE'

you are meshed in mysteries
continually pulling yourself from hats that
are inside locked boxes surrounded
by tanks of clear water
where do you come from
and where, love

the gentle dog trainer pushes aside his empty bowl
there is a yelping from outside, so he goes to the window
he sees Peanuts, the spaniel, writing Provençal pomes
and Ginger, the snapper, etching
and Frowzer, the all dog, concocting a ballet
ah! these dogs are trained, he barks
goes back to the bowl, recently filled

here again the pen, and connected—me
some muses are nubes, like mine
and her commands are like tulips
stalked and banded, she is the prisoner warden
she is owned and owning, herself
the reciprocal dream

be careful! there are kangaroos in the region!
as you walk, they think you are playing
and may hop over you, expecting to be leap-frogged over
or a young 'roo may hop in your pocket
or a mother kang may stick you in hers
in any case: do not panic, kangaroos are friendly
and will not attack unless provoked by absurd truths
once they realize you cannot hop, and cannot fit in or out
they will leave you alone—
expecting the same from you, of course

that he is a professor of language is first
the he cries like a Spaniard in the shower encompasses
   that
so concerned with—he sounds like
that his wife ran off with a Puerto Rican deaf-mute
never knowing that her husband's book was dedicated to
   her
then, he never knew she couldn't read

Wendy is a brown lady and she sings
also her baby, named Wendy
together they live on South Street in New York City
is that any place for two Wendys? caught
between two bridges, offering coffee to passers-by?

you touched me & now
i have a blister there
the swelling will go down
if i lance it
right now, though, i'm enjoying it
kiss it—see if it goes away

the vitamin pills are on parade!
brigades of A and B and C
ah! the complex health pill, the little
save yr life red pills
all to make you what you are
and healthy to boot

*   ***   *

sitting with no food
smoking stale cigarettes, the smoke tasting like vomit
the two poets talk the world
talk poem talk and live poem life
the thick smoke, a triangle bridge,
becomes a haiku
hides the poets' faces connects the two poems

the coal miners sit on porch swings in Harlan, Kentucky
sipping buttermilk or lemonade with mint leaves
singing about miners' strawberries
John L put 'em on strike over twenty years ago
and the owners didn't give in, no sir
they just bought machines or closed up
and coal mining's a pretty specialized trade—
got the smoke and dust in your lungs, ain't much else you
    can do
'cept—sittin' on the porch, swingin',
goin' further and further into yr mind, the black cavern
and pullin' out chunks of blackness

we've begun pulling men out of Viet Nam!
hooray! we shout, yea, the boys are coming home!
only they aren't coming home—they're being sent to the
    Middle East
wars should be fought under supervision of mothers
and all the boys must be *home* by eleven

the All-American blonde girl walks by, carefully averting
that's her style!
many boys stare at her, a few will kiss her
she averts them all
never knowing if anything is really inside her
that is: the sapling greeness of her tongue
when she finally kisses as the French do

                    *   ***   *

the vision appeared again today
of the Man with No Head
rising strangely while i was listening to
a rare raga, and the girl next to me
did not notice me, my suck breath
but i did not applaud. . . .
Christ! he's followed me here
and if he can find me here. . . .

i keep returning to similar sounds
you have been warned
what i really mean is
around me is the echo of a world civilization
all repeating after me, and i in the center
and from my mouth the foreign sounds
the shrieks of the Alaskan witches burn me
and i am repeating the Grand Trial
an innocent in the midst
one woman's love and a solemn policeman
will someone please turn off the shimmering chandelier?

the trees laugh as she garnishes them
and around her twines the only daisy chain
tonight she wll roll the passion-fool ship
then foresake us and return—oh! the ranting rain
the rain—and my forest is alive

i had to talk deep to somebody today, a friend
i feel funny doing it, i'm not sure of me even,
how can i help him, how can i dredge up that love-work
of Meher Baba? but i touched him, and that's a start
he can sleep too, perhaps my covered love can
penetrate the dainty dream, the slipper sound of human
     tears

the growth is a strange music to my head
my head the mushroom, the music a rain chant
the rain the silk cover, it covers the remains
the remains untouchd, the touches are not feared
the fears are growing, that growth, that strange music
to my mushroom head

call him Parsifal, the quester, the outsider
and our laughs MANNA
our segmented selves began the writing
and through it Tiresias begins to slowly close
lots of people they sit and talk about him
but when he comes, so like a Vishnu incarnation
so physical, so frightfully physical, we cannot talk *with*
    him
and like the hounded soul, he sags back into the darkness,
impenetrable, alone, beyond and the great beyond

we had no clothes on and could not make love
we stretched out and her body folded and flexed and mine
    rigid
and her eyes so closed and the grass between us
the soarings of the preparing storm wind and around us
    the gods
parts of the same dream, invented and mutated by our own
    hands
Christ, we are naked, Christ we make no love

a lonely Australian once remarked
that his country offered everything but love
i find this hard to believe, but then i'm as prejudiced as the
    next guy

above me is the roof of mackeral
i crave it, i do
i work my life away and the damn thing
pushes up, pushes up, pushes up
elevating like some frail dancing swordsmen
gutted and rising and i reach the roof
out they swim off, i alone in the great ceiling race
listening to the sea, listening to my parents' god
listening to my own bourgeois soul, wonder
i wonder how to get down, down
and which way, excuse me, which way is home?

as a present, she gave me the Cantos
Ezra the exorcist, ah! blinding chants and cauldrons
i am of the chalk tattoos
the business of that strange man ignites me!
but on the frontispiece is her inscription
and suddenly the impersonal genius opus
is rent into a personal love vendetta
Shui-Te, ah! the love of woman for man, my love's for me,
slight loves, brother, they crack open my whole body

i give birth daily
the hot rock makes me glisten
and from my infernal womb i spread out
the gentle creature, my skin
oh! he look a lot like me!
him be a good boy!
the hard-line Commie tailor with the big cigar
he looks at my love child, he says
'Shit, boy—hee-hee-hee—you better bury 'em quick.
    He ain't even gestated!'

No! No! I am swaying!
the voices warned me, yet i—
what worry now rationalization
i cry! the violence of my bone

'look. i didn't mean anything. we was just playin'.'
'lissen, mister, i could give a goddam. just look at the body
    and—'
'yeah. that's her. O GOD'
'shut the fuck up. you *bastard*! you could care!
'oh man—don't say that—oh man—i do care, o God,
man, you don't—o man, i *loved* her!'

above below
around surround
the ways of men are strange and infinite, aren't they?
and each of us tries to tell each of tries,
and we are sinking under the weight of all these words
and everybody telling, and me worst of all…
oh, i think the time has come,
to begin listening… i wait, wait, smile at you,
people, and, listen!—i listen

oh, you're awake
this is the trial
and this is the riddle
for the living:
	open eyes?
for the dead:
	open eyes?
ultimate choices
we'll roll the roles in turn

with the eyes of the wind around us, we dance
inside the bough smile, in the sea haven
we stash out the sad, clamber aboard, new lungs of joy
all of us morning awake to our bodies
knowing the way, open door
with the eyes of the wind around us, we dance

now the white room, mushy with yogurt floor
barely enough room to breathe, barely room
huddled beneath the lone open bulb, the bulb dripping
	sweat
choose straws to see who dies
someone must leave the room, there is so little air
this, the first sacrifice, the muscle push out the flap door
birth, the yogurt tissue latch, the vanished room

blessed America, i cry as i enter
another nickel in the coin slot
there was social security in the Nazi SS, too, i believe
in Africa the tom-drums send news you can dance to
back to dark Adams, your family has stood on fathers'
    shoulders
to put you where you
and there you are

that great womb-escape
your brain slurped into
the head encasement, peering out of two little holes
look on down for surprises
yes, a body too, for running around
it seem to be going somewhere
you come to

and i slip my tongue up under my upper lip & i see
lip hairs! my very own lip covered by hair forest!
acknowledged: i am bearded
but the excitement of hairs there. . . !
come, explore your body
the representative map becomes the actual land

see the tree surrounded by people sea
they sail over the roots and under the limbs
the tree accents them, accepts lovers' carvings
accepts dog offerings
accepts bottles in its crevices
rather nonchalent, this tree, about those things?
not really—just that all its tree energy goes up into
bouying up the sky...

the maker of the wonderful bubble machine sadly
    scratches his ear
for years the demand for bubbles has been decreasing
this year the funds are so low that
HE CANNOT AFFORD BUBBLE-MAKING FLUID
if only bubble parties would come back into vogue . . . .
but no, best pack up the ol' machine
start selling gum, blow your own

she spangles at him, black and gold
he starts slow flashes, black and green
the voltage ups and ups
but its still the checker game, black and red
she moves   he moves
alternating   current

i walk into the room, find a lover with my lady
he is over her, head buried
i stand shock still
i watch them, she coos
their bodies are original jazz
he lifts his head—it's me!
it's just that i've been for a little walk
i've been for a walk inside her

dragonfly priest busy
administering to white clover drops
skimming over holy water
natural ceremonies symbolic
man with his arm at elbow, extending nail wounds
life mirrors life, the necessities become the history
dulled history becomes myth
a fortune of myth is dragonfly

today the Italian record seller was called a 'curly-headed
    chump!'
immediately goes on diet of cottage cheese and celery
skinny and virile, he'll sell more records
maybe a lady Bach-buyer will ask him home
to listen to the new stereo
then the boss will give him a raise
he could marry and settle down—
settle down to the cottage cheese, don't waste a curd!

everybody is somebody you know
glance at a stranger—there, wasn't that _____?
now stare at him—well, no, not him,
but it does look sort of like _____
there you are, surrounded by people you know!
now look in the mirror—there are two of you
thanks to people and mirrors there's no loneliness

that night Ernie pulled a knife on me and the police came
roaring up to this Harlem tenement ready to open fire
discovering me hand to head
and Ernie directing Handel with a dull butcher knife
Ernie, forgotten actor/writer, this epistle is for you
i heard they threw you in the drunk tank to sober up
anyway, you left you sweater behind

mouth chatter chatter over diamond teeth
this sidewalk is glittering under street lamp lighthouse
the scene is set for the jetty couple—here
they are! she red-haired and furry, he tanned a bronze
but she is so drunk, oh
she get sick on pavement
the mouth hole open for a decade, flows
snaps shut; that diamond square is put out
lighthouse beams blackness to the passing vessels

by the creek toddles the young boy, now adventurer
he knows the least, so enters the water with bare feet
on a raft, sailing to the string stream
a tributary that fingers into the mud river, where he
    capsizes
into the sea, the balm salve
and beneath the sea, the sea

God cries the 19th century man, the Mexico life!
a clean-shaven sun and frankly Margueritas
the woman and her salt-drink namesake
they coddle my body, a bottle of each
lips hold firm the glass of one, while lips in lips of the other

addendum: to people who have stoves, please
take care of them, you cook on them and in them
if you aren't hospitable and concerned, the heat will collect
your stove will melt
love being the best energy easer

the turtles have turned and gone back
moving cairns, moss heaped, the life retreat
and the sun comes up and the sun comes down
the extraneous sun and day and time
the forever crawl and i want

clouds move
they are calcified smoke
from some great briar pipes in Kiev
the bells too glisten and send messages from bronze
the naked natives and this woman
crying under the purge weight
her family marrow split, she had pleaded her belly
now the swelling has moved up to her head
she is alone, with her head

'did you see that? did you see that?'
'no'

*   ***   *

i, too, have danced the pixy dance
adorned in a sow's mask, snorting my humanity
wow, am i clumsy!
i move my feet only to trip over my feet
and my hands play up my body to my neck
my eyes will not be open
what is happening at my loins?
little pins of laughter, my mask jets off, i weep

what shall i do, Michael Wood?
realizing my position & unaware of any potential,
i'll go the road route, the profane pilgrimage
can i visit you in the moors? speak Spanish with your wife?
us and Sterne there with the banshees
i'll bring the curtains and you bring the wine
i'll drop by for a visit, yes
the journal of the American traveler is endless and
    encapsulated

she is worried
she not speak English so good
she say, it sound pretty, like music
she say, it sound funny
in Brazil, though, it is summer all the time
there, no need for words
music, i suppose, suffices

well, we're all in this together, so we might as well laugh
2,000 years of God headed civil-i-zation
& we still pick our noses
you should read about Freud and jokes
every time we laugh, we are laughing at our own human
    condition
what a bore perfection would be, so awfully cozy
let's get a belly full and then explode—
barrels of belly guffaws

begone sir! she'd shout to the hook peddlar

he' d skidaddle away, his passel of hooks clinking and
matted

they're hand-in-hand, having come
to me with news of themselves
i knew them each alone before
they came together over me
i was lying alone in the green meadow i had shared at
    times
with them both, though separately
it was my secret birthday, so i was taking a secret birthday
    nap
but they crept up on me from either side
carrying cakes for me
me, they didn't see,
instead, a mirror reflecting the other
love was theirs as i lay napping in the meadow
now they come to tell me of it
i nod as if knowledgable, actually still dreaming

the peace of the warrior sat down hard
invited to this sissy dinner party
aughta be out a-crackin' skulls, he thought portly
instead bang into the roast beef
his loincloth and bronze belt medallions, now
they were a strange poem themselves
yet he ate, and the other guests, having
heard of his presence, failed to show
such things the peace of warrior doesn't notice
are most amazing to his enemies

the twelve cut off their arms at elbow
to form the astrologic dividers
like rivers, they stretch to the farmhouses
hands forming wavy waves of the zodiac
clabbering, growing black and finally thin as lines
pointing at once to the star, to the unborn child, the star

led like huskies, the children who have no brains
are pulled on the yearly field trip to the dust museum
the teacher has them bagged
and he lectures (Here, Turk dust. But *there*, Bulgarian
    dust!)
don't hold water, not
that it matters (really) anyway
the baby boys will be bad
the baby girls will be troublesome
chained, there's probably one brain among them

four sheepherders, one curly and three straight
all the four go for one sheep! they
will guide him home with love
the bleat sheep is a good half-mile off, so they all go
they leave the flock in loaves, safe
and tramp off
       (will they come back? are they right in doing this?
          do sheep
       understand? do the sheepherders understand? can
          we, waiting
here in loaves, understand?)

black as boils, the volcano pimples
do dot the whole of Iceland
here, the funny-faced women live the apple-gnome legends
there is the one about the strange traveler
and there is the one about celery seed cake
and many others
not to depress them, but the volcanoes are burping
then, the people of Iceland have lived with this for
    centuries
    (especially the women)
they are used to it now, and have forgot time

last train just flickered past
i see on it the girl whose parents told me, 'watch out for
    her'
i did—i just saw her go
she smiled at me, i don't think she would have smiled at
    them

at midnight, the midnight guru turns over in his sleep
hence his name, as in you
with no name, turning over so rarely
a one hundred year flower spins out the long life 'til
    blossom—
you have just finished a quarter-turn

from here to there is two things (you say):
one—to decide to go there
two—the act of going—there!
why then, can i be beside you (while not)?
and, as long as we're one the subject,
going there means passing by the creek, doesn't it? also
    trees?

this then can be the part of the flying goat
have you seen it?
ate too much you know
and everybody told it
wouldn't listen
eventually and in one generation, mutated
strange puttings, finally flew
—ate too much you say

whenever i think of the lady as Helen
i know i'm just seeing the Yeats at work in me
is it so horrible to be satisfied in love?
must love be masochistic as all that?
these are the question for him
Helen i may see my lady as, but only for me, without aid or
    solace

his mouth opens & out comes the noise
it is the pain of the shock of discovering you are
in that part of the tableau, that
part in the lower left corner
that part where the fellow gets the sword right through the
    stomach gut

down hard against the rail, the standing spectators
will have fence pressure marks against their chests
they stand through no effort, straightened by the multitude
    behind
stock cars bang around past them once in a while
eyes dart to discover the winning number
inside each car is a human, fighting with the wheel
mile after circular mile, faster than thinking
inside each driver, bloodstream flows
mile after circular mile, towards the black-white checkered
    flag

Jingle John talks in rhyme, sells the news all night
searches the ground for dropped pennies
a man buys a paper, finds it inside the rhyme
'Here's the paper for you tonight, Hope you find
    everything's all right'
lurking inside his poetry are the vile ink wars
hiding inside his pockets are pounds of dropped pennies

o me, to sit here w/ shaking hands
baby i'm ready for it all
i could blow the society and retire now
grow younger with the years
a synopsis of the bastard son: original Bozo

this end up, perishable, handle with care
books are monosexual, this one keeps pushing
the hoi phalloi determinants
never seen in nature, the imprint decal of AUTHOR'S
 NAME on each forehead
go to sleep in the ultraviolet light
bones' x-ray awake, canceled,
too long standing—on your head—you are peeling your
 skull

horses and bluebirds, served by the farmer Belgium
a low country, eked out
there are hoary children here, already goitered
the happiness of a furrowed brow only man could endure
if the fingers could move, that fat bread could be dunked in
 mud coffee
as it is, beards are pulled from mothers' wombs
the animals and fowl certainly would survive anyway
but then how would the Belgians get calloused? do for a
 living?

aftermath of last night (you were here)
gives me something to do
i swab the spilt wine, throw out the candle puddle
between my fingernails capture the black ash matches
no way, though, there is no way
to rid this room of your river fragrance
quotation marks stand sentry at the window

guilt

damn this race!

try to hide you and me under hair, no use

i press white into my fingernails, but sans pressure pink
   blood returns

(Granny says i was such a cute baby and so pink)

scrub scrub with soap, no use

as a caucasian i sit guilty in the stocks

my body forms a [, the martyr

so guilty that to martyr me only intensifies that guilt

and the damn cleansings of hair and soap leave me only
   more naked
      and all the more laughable

please, if you have any suggestions at all

don't send them off to your country home

to be sheared with the cube bushes

let 'em play in the streets of this city

wow, will shout a little boy bouncing your plan,

do *i* have an idea!

thank you, save the world

*   ***   *

oh! Holman is sad, he
has pulled deep down inside him now
his mind abounds with externals (what to do with her?)
when the matter is with him
will he pull himself up?
or will he stay cowering, making that movie of himself?
this chunk of reality might stay with him
this, the first day of September, this 1969 of now

drat and bother
love no more than a mosquito bite
it shrives the skin tissues
lump ache in the unscratchable area
right beside the mind

boy found dead
on the roof of this building (four ceilings above)
15 and brown
scream still locked on his face
needle still locked in the bloodless vein

Ralph had his chance and he blew it
at his age it's only a question of trying too hard
was it really a mistake when he pulled his Ford
out in front of the milk truck
which whore was it that night, Ralph
whose baby cried too loud

calligraphy is an art

see these word-worms on the page

once they were parcel of my personality

and now they belong to a union typesetter (just as good)

while making the Chinese character for HAPPINESS,
   SoChing stops and

chews the pen tip. if she were not writing, she would bite
   her nails.

she lived at a fashionable address 30 years ago, never
   moved

she has grown old, now in her 70's

her face has changed, she has changed

you cop smack on her doorstep

it's not so fashionable there anymore

but she still wears white gloves when she goes out

and nods to the doormen as she comes home

the low music from the Russian room seeps like smoke

in there are the two men

some kirsch, some cigars, some music

these are the slow hatchings of the plot

and the grand finale: chilled vodka held in the mouth 'til
   warm

will burst on us in an army of men

to skin an orange you first puncture the peel with a
   fingernail

the Russians hold the globe in their palms

who knows who the eaters will be, the destined pulp-
   eaters are?

Izzy walks at night to the phone booth
in the late night, it beams as an oasis
clenched in his hand is the sliver silver dime
he reaches the glass haven, shut out the world
he has reached his decision
money slotted, two bings, the tone, the seven digits
his fingers move slowly as they carve out the call
she will be home, or not
frantically the buzz sound jets across the city
the sleeping lady awakes to the last round bell, stumbles to
    the phone

gingersnaps for breakfast?
care to ignore the boy, my dear
he ain't pregnant, just ignorant
never amount to much, anyhow
feed him what he wants, i guess
better eat his dinner, though
better down them veggies

if i granted you the wish, would you take it?
what would the wife say
take a piece of heart again, baby
blow out the candle
the ashes cradle your new-born ass's head
your adam's apple has clogged in the loneliness
and drinking and pissing are no purge at all

gonna ease up
take it
as it is
not ask for
nothin' and tomorrow ain't
gonna open up
these damn eyes at all

hmm, you say you take drugs, ooo
do you hallucinate? or just feel drowsy?
have you ever slept while 'tripping'? balled?
does it heighten your experiences?
do you have experiences?
do you experience?
do you?
do?
would you say that Hamlet that cat sees the same things
    you do?
normally?

gitar man, rag the slow tune
i am not the man i used to be
i cannot be, don't want to be
my body's gone gristle, my beard's here to stay
the lady's a memory, the silks put away
oh, gitar man, rag the slow tune
& listen to your words & that makes 'em true

wrinkles on the man's legs
the evil beasties of varicose veins en route to his knees
can you be rich and bandied; well, he is
if he could only lay a dozen in a week
if he could, he'd plant that sunflower
he'd show them all
if he could
if he only could

the bitterer the memories (she'd say) the more pungent the
    dream
she'd scream
they were (her family) lost in a fire
('lost?' 'no, killed. burned.')
she blows up her body (balloon) in mornings
afternoons, the air hisses out on the bus from work
she hangs her limp self up in the bedroom closet
lays herself out, pressed, (empty) for the next day

'did you have a nice time this summer?'
'yes'
'did you go away?'
'yes. i went away to the country'
'was it nice there?'
'yes, it was. it was nice away in the country where i went
    this summer.'

kaleidoscope, complete with variations
arrives on your doorstep today
invited in, the show will go on forever
kicked out, the show will go on forever
such gifts come in strange packages
this one comes unwrapped
ready for immediate use,
congratulations! you're a WINNUH!
used immediately

in this boy scout shirt, he looks as much like Gnossos as
    anyone
the spirit is there, but the novel has been worn
his ears are dogged pages, his blistery feet the lone
    compromise
he should've forsaken motorcycles
he was much loved, no
yes, he is much loved

the bombing stops
in the earth's bowels the vibrations heave one last time
the mystic and his loved sip from the wine jug
the sowing is done now
on the barren earth the reaping begins

darkness and darkness
black night silence
she can leave the hole, finally
walking on silent toes, carrying the hatchet
at last to the hill, where hanged on the tree
her cracked-neck husband dangles
his crime: he believed in no God
she will bury him by the bridge where they first made love
      above his grave the black shaped-fire
      a fitting burial for an atheist, he had once mused
      is to be covered with earth, and just left
she throws that last dirt on his body, accordingly, and
   leaves

this, shrieks the teacher, is the BIG STORY
listen—or else!
the children listen to the story that
the teacher had listened to
they listen closely, so they can repeat it
outside, the mysterious two snuggle a ciggie butt
chuckle between split teeth

green on brown
this is a poem of season's change
there are seasons for us, it seems
can i help my wrinkled ways
can you be other than young
there are times in bed when i feel summer between us
a clean wind burst
but tonight i felt ice breasts
you frozen atop me
for the longest moment we stayed like that
i watched a whole season pass over your body
you changed green to brown
finally,
as it happens with leaves

*   ***   *

another music now: piper's flute
calling—no, not calling—
sounding the tone of the day
leaving you where you are, but enriched
i am sitting on the pocked beach
sounds: gulls, waves, sun setting vacuum rush,
lady's fingernails scratchy my cheek
under and above and in them all
the wily piper wails
pumped up by the day lungs themselves

invisible, she crosses herself
warding on God, the dusty fellow
were there eyes to see her, they would crown her
on her head though is bandage
her brother sits beside her
(can't see her, doesn't know she sees him)
he's waited since the accident, there
inside the mummy wrappings now
angels trip in triumph, the new saint has knelt

th' man, he's flaccid
he's a-old & he's a-fallin' down
like the bum, man, that ev'budy said (always said) he'd be
why sure, 'n a bit drinky-punch drunk
at the moment, and a-rollin' it off
down by the train station
'O!' my God, the sun's a a-comin' up!
'n the 6:15'll roll in—God, the lonely whistle's still drivin'
        in my head'

smoking a tipped cigarette
the Swiss banker cycles through Bern to his office
when finished, the cigarette filter will be put in his pocket
not for saving's sake, but sanitation
like his precious paws thumbing and indexing numberless
    unnumbered accounts
with the broom lady humming at 3 francs per room—
cleanliness is next

this too, the desert mountain black
and silt sand, battered iron speckles
and the tin piano chant of Tibet
there, the most advanced 'country' in the world…
600,000 species of insects, 242 species of mammals
who, God, becomes the value judge?
how advanced the lonely mountain?
the horn of power rests uneasy in the breast of man

born on the Vineyard, sailed out in the Merchant Marine
got the scar (stupid fight, actually) in Jo-burg
back to the Vineyard and the girl with thin legs
hard fat drop to ankles—but married 'er, yup
now fixes pumps an' things, neck still a copper cobra
eyes still like gulls—yes i guess they are

*   ***   *

'goo, man! Reformation, foogie
dwadle a sound cent years—oof!'
youth —old as our eyes are taught
to see and read
and ears obey too
my god they've done it to us and even
revolution becomes one game in one (political) sphere
and even love cannot humanize some
'belief, in periods of war, is harder than bullets,'
repeated over every dying soldier, priest finding unguent
    goo
in his brillantine bristled, now red matted, skull
amen

back up, the diver
appears, face joy as the blow fish
disappearing as the salt melts it
and floating on the wave
a smile
a fish go free
and the final mermaid, dancing with ocean gods, Circe
    avec trident

she sits cross-legged intent
in the house with the glass roof
the fog it does pour down like sun
she in the strange light, purple in her body
casually throws off a lover, a book page, nude leaf

dipping, another life stirred up
realize the power of relating
word-bomb lifted into individual Hiroshima
oh! the war is lost in hearts my friend
all's fare in love and war
later, the plot sickens, something blocks,
heart death as real death

the Great God bends down again again again
lower to meet pulls off the cover
the ever-laugh God, Baal, spruced up
and out on the town
in our bellies he kicks like a babe
outside and dapper, we recognize him as
force
a life on the rudder
he smells of living
and dies so far away, the corpse cannot be smelled at all

i turn to pale ghost in the presence of two
they down brown bourbon in bowls, so no matter
am i sulking or skulking?
they talk of dog breeds and value judgement
on the other side of spaghetti, my shotgun bears down
right on the nose! no escape!
i will not yield i have already yielded
even as hunkering ghost by the velvet table
i am sighing compromises
the pacifist lays down the horrid weapon
guts drunk

as a sculptor his mind refuses
to acknowledge similarity of 'building up' and 'carving out'
so he turns to mechanic or craftsman
sock down his fears
packs up his yurt on North Shore
kisses all the Cambridge yeomen bye bye

dearie, dearie—don't touch me now
times when a woman best be alone
(that's me, the woman)
and now, dearie with my brains bangin'
and nothin' turnin' out, well…
kiss me, kiss me!

no meddling
leave alone
so many become old farts on busses
straining to overhear, to read the letter over the shoulder
sticky fingers attracted to everything
once that final mousetrap is built
we must learn how to speak it
catch those ears with stringent gossip
and a big mousetrap on their big nose

who will e'er forget (now that i'm reminded)
that joyous super subway ride, drunk as a fart's ass
buffaloing it underground NY with Evan
reading the Parable of Sweet Grace, the center we enter
    through
on the Great White Bed
and Evan disappearing at the 14th St. station
teeth gritting, not knowing if i'd e'er make it home
not knowing if i'd remember ol' Gracie

mangy, mangy—won't ze dog (*pliz*!) quit pissink on ze
    floor!
where has she gone, too
the bull fiddle throws her heavy spiritual on the city
people pass
time, too, passes
in its fashion

crickets herald this verse
and the man hears them
his are not the cricket symbols
but simple ones, rustic
thirty years of beard
reared and now alone in West Virginia
alone? well…
who say alone?
the crickets—but they are with him
the frogs—but… them too
ok, the baron leans back in his rocker
surveys his populace, mighty lord of the manor

it's all in how you look at it
will Zimmy ever use the eyes of Glo?
the ascent the apex of degradation
wander among crap-shooters and pimps
burn fleshy arm joint with cigarettes
smear body-crap on newest face-mask
reductio ad absurdum
to fell all, you must have felt all
to be, you must have been
the search to be the lowest common denominator

forgotten wars spread out of historics
no longer to be memorized by high school leaders
every once in a while some new graveyard
will yield some new numbers
deciphered by scholars, this new discovery
will herald a new age

lullabye, my baby
let me pull down the lids
softly, and so very smooth
that one point between my big thumb and clumsy indexer
let me touch you
touch you to bed
the naked touch
of your naked touch
on my naked
touch

you will recognize me by the flower in my buttonhole
i will recognize you by the boots that cover your knees
we will make love that night
and travel years until we climax
how strange now, that one night
how covered and muddled and complex things have grown
the mysteries of then, love,
the unveiling?

*   ***   *

again? again again
the softest possible tune eases around my brain
as a cover, it covers the headless image, the mirrored
    sidewalk love
as a scout, it shouts the break dawn of a new cycle
now, though, it is satisfied with itself alone
walking the fantasy thin-line
between actual and mocking of the actual
and again again lodges itself
for the rest
invincibly armored, my strange melody, the miracle of me

her clock breaks
she buy another one
the car won't start
she junk it
the toaster burn out
she hold bread and bare breast to sun
all in all, she's a consumer
channeled into needs
the needs mold her being
as gross therefore as she is, the grotesqueness is a replica
as she is, all in all, your very own replica

this boy looks in me in the body, i cannot look him in the
    eye
what look is that: pure love, pure body love
he is slicked so, almost perfumed
and his voice low, enticing—hollow
i have to look away to speak my scratchy words
lumber heavy off to excuses
my sweat fears in his eye oceans

he defines love as 'mutual continuous positive
    reinforcement'
and makes his wife the same way
the egg-timer buzzes at the end of foreplay
he is inside her within the next minute
they bang around then for a while
hit a slow sea rhythm
soporific
finally easing into Nodding into
he hasn't come in years, & she's Pavlov-trained for sleep at
    the buzzer
the jelly penis sleeps in the dry hole, the shrink

man, he laugh so good through a few yellow rock teeth
in his own store, dancin' about
slappin' ice cream balls into brown crunch cones
'what you want—a double!' and
clitters away, soft shoed toe back step left
the chocolate mounds he can build!
his own store, and Arnold his son
stares baby-eyed from the stroller
unbelieving of the man his father
the toothless cream clown of Lenox Ave

a poster of three owls nailed to the wall, framed by book-
    cases, books, conch shell
she's a med student, he's a 6th grade teacher
they toss words between the two couches
the girls inject a comment, with total apostrophe
i sit on a brown chair, preturbed when i'm asked if i'm first-
    born
retorting how Pisces i am
really wanting to be the owl in the middle, the one with
    green eyes

thick as goose neck
fingers curl pistol's bone handle
holster leather-grease
left hand to mouth, flick throw down butt
crush with two boot twists
non-blinking eyes
dust rise and settle rise
trigger finger gunman
even the dust swirl
is too much
where is the action? when
is the movement?
account for that
we are all accountable

tomorrow tomorrow
prepared in chuckles, the wealth lode
the rich cache awaits
and how did it get there
and why does it wait to spring open?
i regress

accepted at the bar, leaning on it
downing neat scotches, glass and all
another day—five ways to say that
and two days to complain of it
a tacit touch to tie and all
another drink slips on down
the bald bartender, stomach caving over his apron
wipes brew off bar
sets up another round
new customer
the ghosts change places

a fresh plastic disc, pressed but ungrooved
punched like a record, playable on a record player
but the needle, not catching, can only zip from edge to
    center, edge
to center
eventually (there are many years in this parenthesis), the
    needle will make a slight scratch
later still (years later), the scratch will elongate
(your sons' sons will be replacing the turntable's motors by
    this time)
finally, the disc will be completely grooved
and that will be a record, my friends
a record of it all

DO YOU DEFINE MY REALITY?

TIME WARP

DO YOU DEFY MY REALITY?

i wanna riot like early Arab poets, cameling around
maidens covering our footprints with sand-scratching
   nightgowns
the tough days to the far-off oasis
the cold nail desert nights, wolf-sentried
as for the next day, i do na' care
as for death, i wanna rot

boy this day's got me
strung-out
my two fingers pressure down on the desk
my arm's a rod
to my shoulder balanced over back of chair
chair standing on two legs
held by my thrust-out legs
toes point press the floor
there's a pen in my mouth
i write this poem on paper
hanging loosely
from a string
nailed to
ceiling

the candle queries
the magician, rubbing his palms off, is active in waiting
'shamilar, ondāgo'
he repeats the words
crescendos with the flame
slackens with the flame
it is not the magic we know of, dream of
these are the curses of cairds
the white aura classes us aristocrats
his hand, at last red worn, cups
the flame, puffs off the flame, black

Diana Sara has never seen an August
too busy with summer to particularize
she lifts us up, unbothered by bees or past bees
hmm, she plays on flowers,
walking over them, not touching them, trailing them
    behind her
her man, the youngest of beards, has crowned her
queen of August
she knows him, knows not what it means

'hey, i'm sorry i'm later...'
'that's ok, i expected it.'
'what do you mean?'
'well, it's typical, isn't it?'
'yes, and your *saying* that is typical, too!'
'yes.'

*   ***   *

the goulash knave, waxing his nose hairs
flattening his belly-beginnings, cocking
on the red bowl hat, man he's
set to occupy the ville!
young maidens, ah take heed the word
the world it's ablaze with amber lights (caution!)
he's taking the nose count, con-man's census
and tonight, mes petites, he'll snarl the whip position, i.e.
     fop's atop

is it appropriate
in this section (to the lady) to give a thank-you
for the gift of plastic fruits in bowl?
well,—black squirrel in back lot, my room with toys
     hanging,
feather still plaited in your hair, my hair grease from lack
     of 'poo—
step up! (the barker) three chances for a dime, even more
     for a quarter
aye, the rumblings from the peasant mob, seeking wildly
     Doc Frankenstein
he's breathing heavy, sitting next to me in my room, wow
     scared
bathed in the light of, pink-like glow,
emanating (i bow, plus: smile) from
the plastic bowlful

i'm picking up the piano
so many have already done it!
    ('well?' 'ok, right, like the pounder upstairs')
my sister, 12 already does it, scaling and annoying
my little brother (Peej) has been shown off on certain
    young Christmases
playing 'Hark! etc.' and singing boy soprano gilt
me, i'd like to tear into a red rag 'Mamie!' number (mood of
    moment)
later to flip me tails back over the stool
screw it up 'til my ten equal its 88
hair flow and humming like Gould i'd vary the variations to
    suit
all this dependant on my ability to concentrate past the
    stool
round up down, like the drugstore ones in New Richmond
feet kicking me around past the coke and hands greasy as
    warm butter from popcorn

don't, friend, shatter the ruse when
a quotes poor beggar end quotes halts and
asks you for that bus money (twice times too dear) to
visit his dying soon-gone barely abreath step-aunt
ah, that moment as real for you two as the next with your
    own
treated kind, glass intact, life is breathed for that
    communion instant
pay, man, or don't pay for that privilege
creating that diologue, filling that between-space with
    substance
as real as the sidewalk you've stopped on
let him be—build—man,
don't break down

frozen and locked
she is religion personified
quartz eyes, granite chin, steel nose
her body is a column
thick
her God is so demanding that He gives her all
His narrow way becomes the super-highway
she alone knows it and rolls down it
like Columbus, only she rolls off the edge

the sun shines brightly, Nate is not fooled
this is the winter, people will want his cab
to escape from snow and to hustle packages
well, he'll do it
and in his mind he won't see streets at all
but driving over virgin moss country
and the people in the back will disappear
and he'll tan finally—'never cold in the country'
he wises them up
until the light changes

'which way bud?'
'uptown'
'sorry, can't go uptown'
'why not?'
'my wife lives up there. if i run into her, she'll kill me'
'well, do you really think we'll run into her?'
'hope not. i don't have any insurance'
'hey,—i'm an insurance salesman!'
'hop in !'

cops in jeep
disappear down St. Mark's subway
2 cops on cop-scooters follow them
a blaring cop across 8th, cop heavies out & down
coupla cycles, blue helmets bobble off, disappear
soon, all right-yellow flush lights
the air's a grease block of REAL and HERE & NOW
i walk on
it's all part of the plan

stupid to conserve
it dies inside of you
eats away while you live
and clots up when you die
like the black pitch in the hash smoker's pipe, karma
opiate by any other name

night in the concert hall
on the stage is Mauger, alone in loaf clothes
crowing his bassoon, practicing for the 'Firebird'
high and eerie, the opening's his solo
his cigarette smolders on the music stand,
waiting for a few bars' rest
the tenor sounds tease over the empty hall
then fermata: hold hold hold
this single pitch the essence of it all
rising like a demon, the bird takes flight

the Frowzer ballet
fiddles and horns with arpeggios
she spots the pot and arrabesques about the hydrant
as! pas de deux with it
pirouette now (enter violas in counter-point)
i cannot enter the dance now, nor you
nervous under our collar, leashed to the apropos
sans dog suits, we're naked with Saks on
and Frowzer, concocting madly now
(flugelhorns, clarinets, oboe and cello)
lifts up his left rear leg salute

young boy turns artist

directs himself into confrontation with the beast

doesn't know it's behind him

edged off into the Real World

no, not that one, he's too secure there

over here, no; there—no, behind the potted plant!

here, hold this lad, this globe

and juggle it with these, old buddy: pens & bows & sticks &
lime

watched by the single audience:

a girl, waiting patiently and quietly, remarkably silent, sans
applause

until he beings dropping his props

capsizing us all

into her empty mind

that was not right

he shouldn't have done that

as a parent apparent i move him back

behind his son's son

and in the morning ah!

i'll awake him then, lily o la!

and trot him up again

until he does it right

wait! cries the Thai spice merchant
you've forgotten your change --
but the cry (alas!) is lost in the paprika
and the lady customer, wrapped in ginger sugar
has palmed a lapful of cloves anyway
o! the Thai, they know how to work it out
equitably

he won't come back
he's rolled the soldier, for Brecht's sake
and strapped on the coilless and gear
we can count them: mother, father, girl, plus assorted more
    distants
mother: he'd grown, i was childless anyway
father: pro patria (chuckle) means 'dad' too, eh? or have i
    forgotten the declensions?
girl: i told him
soldier-lover-son:

15 years of marriage
'something happened today'
'i'm glad'

i just don't understand these bites on my body
oh surely i must go like some charming prince in search of
THE CINDERELLA GIRL WITH THE RIGHT TEETH
these teeth will fit in
molars, eye-teeth (eye-teeth?), cuspids and bi- and incisors
into these marks on me
they could line up now, lips taut to bare them
enamel and all and i don't know if i like this
i don't understand it, waiting nervous for the right hour
when we all begin changing forms

the sorry but standing H addict
slobbered and nodded his way up to me
(just picked me out, i wasn't trying to look receptive)
and said: 'man, for a quarter the secret of the world'
knowing a bargain, i doled it out
'Blop' he whispered, 'is it, and if that doesn't work,
     double Blop'
so Blop and Blop Blop
(i guess something is lost in translation)

here, take a look at *my* teeth
um, yummy-nums, the triple-lensed periscope dentist
he adjusts his view to mouth-size
he rhapsodizes and ruminates
whistles and gears down *TO* drill
dental litany: ' it's better by far not to brush at all
than to brush sideways'

old man happy
been liberated by youthful friends
they take him on as guru, as
their living antique
he flows cultured insanity through his beard
is loved
and then, like watching a movie frame by frame,
three policemen take him, shouting, away
and at the precinct station the desk sergeant laughs,
'oh, him, yeah. Doc? well, ...he's been psychoed.'

when she smiles it's sad
she had that power
she has that power of mine
where she creates what she needs
and you see it because she believes it
she will sit in silence pool for hours
until everyone worries at her, and what's the matter
she is smiling inside
that's where the biggest poem of all is

*   ***   *

blank page stare at me again
like hitch-hiking
'cause you can wait hours & hours
and still sing 'cause
you know somewhere breaking straight at you
is The Ride
& you don't know who it is, or where going
but The Ride's a-comin'
& so i sing

psst. publisher's talk.
can't take this. you know.
i thought (seriously) that this sort
of talk went out years ago. well,
for goodness' sakes! i been soapin' words for
years and now you tell me--
i do declare, you whippersnapper, fiddlesticks!

oh, the librarian is glinting again
she's puttered back into History, American and
cleaned her jewelled glasses on an easy hem
her lover's come in
she prays he is
they do kiss, though, back there
and she gasps as his claws tickle her
oh, she can't laugh her love-laughs here
'don't!' hissed many times
and finally, bald and wrinkling and a teacher for 30 years,
    he
pulls his own lower lip full over his teeth
and bites down in sweat

'expand. expand.
expand. stretch.
stretch.'
(this is your mind talking.)
'i'm bored. i've been channeled and now zip
zip zip the same stimuli
the same way, why?
make-a me smile! i'm-a Italian, now, yousa hear?
open. wide. stretch. growl.
let's-a play!'
—this message was brought along with help from Author.
(' he needs-a alluh the help he's gon' get!')

at last, El Khizr, the green one!
green's life, you know that
also: E.K. knows that you know that
so he slides along in dis -
guises, most recently unknowable as
The Big Green Monster who covers you
olive and emerald and an off-chartreuse
and BGM=EK in essence as he howls big laugh
at life, his most hilarious nightmare

'winks out'
wow, god, i mean everybody
seems to be writing pomes about 'winking out'
and it gets to be first funny and then boring
and then it bugs me. 'winks out' is schmaltz
it's like when i was 12 and my
Sweetheart Evelyn yelled at me for kissing her in
the cloak room at Pierce School and i just stomped on
out of that dark coat-suffocating cloak room
and slammed the door buddy and she just 'winked out'

two by two
is a bored size too

name all the people you know

let's start with this part
ok, let's talk about me.

now, let's talk about this part.
let's talk about you.

ok.
now let's talk about the part in between

*   ***   *

heavy-box lifter with criss-crossed arms
yes, he waits the move instructions
then, like electric drill, bends forwards
to the rope bound box of secrets
snaps the V up
shoulders the load off
the forearm says Move and watches the lift
and waits and cooly thinks
the next command

'please, Mr. Noah, you gonna let me in?'
'can't do that, son—you ain't got the Faith'
'man, i got all the Faith, man. shit, it's rainin' cats & dogs
    out here!'
'son, you aughta see what it's doin' in *here!*'

the lady frowns—her head hurts
take an aspirin
no good more pills
takes kissin' (i get up to do the kissing job)
but as her forehead's kissed, her mouth gets jealous
and attention there leaves her nose alone
her ears cry
and her breasts are lonely
(i can't even begin to think of the pain lower down)
wish i was a poet, have a million mouths
so i become a poet and my whole body's kissing

Eric's anxious with his loneliness
derived from the noise in his head, like spray
could the noise be removed, then he could hear it all
it is like this: real watch an insect
as it climbs up a rock it takes an attitude of climbing
'i know i can climb this rock!' so
it does, one leg at a time, feeling for the edge, hitting,
staying solid. leg leg leg leg leg leg. up that rock.
that is how loneliness is penetrated.
the noise is sucked off, the top of the rock = you --
and then compassion,
remember, it is harder for humans.
we only have two legs.

all right, all right, that's good
now   hold it!—there, that's the pose,
freeeeeze—hold it
there
your hands gripping the book, loose
ready to flip to the next page
eyes wanting to get on with it
hungry mind
words is no camera, buddy
so i *don't* have you
YOU'VE GOT THE BOOK THOUGH
ah ha!
(there. now that was a better shot.
much more natural.
much more—alive.)

your/our friend, your/our pal!
ah, looming in, he is on the horizon
he is breathing energy box—sparks flash off him
rays arrow right into him
sometimes the strange chemistry of his body
makes him ash grey, next to invisible
other times he will be so huge
he folds over, himself, and folds that over-folds --
lost in the folds are his thousand names
flickering in his chemical eye-shutters are his thousand
    images
his neck pulls in,
the sun shuts on his shoulders
and, on his shoulders, there sets a sun

*   ***   *

Spring was the melted butter.
The elephants would remember India.
Bodies loosed like slack plastic.
Mellow sun ball, rays like hair, elbowed the day.
Books were begun and lovers made contact contracts.
After dug-in winter, it was slosh out of mud-cement
    footprints.
Summer would beat us inside.

now all at once i am crying
i stand on the line
where the water breaks off at my ankles
this is foam surf, bringing in black-blue mussels
the she shells are behind
and the ocean is in front
down my face the tears
up my legs the salt spray
and between all this, somewhere, is me
i have become the edge itself
i have become the needle and am pointing

well, i woke up and first
saw the water (the sea is just outside)
then i felt your hand covering my body
then i felt the cool pillow
then the sun began spilling on me
today i knew was the day i'd go
i don't know, sometimes you have to leave
goddamn, you get that Copenhagen feeling, and then you
    have to leave

cold shock
leave the fire
and set out again
>there's the simple way and the complex way
>the easy way and the hard way
>the good way and the bad way
the ways are all parallel
they've all been charted, and the maps wait at the end
sit, burn
travel—learn
they've all been done, and even the way-out way out
is still a way
away

ply you with promises? not my style
live it with you, though
wait and see, i'm the one for that
laughs a-plenty, and sad—there's room for that, too
not even these poems are meant to ply—
but to dance to
just to hold close for a time
then a sigh as the clench ends
and then just some sort of strange
goodby hello

stop. go back.
re-read.
here, you forgot these, the eyes
they have plopped down here
put them in the right way/
or else watch the inside of your mind

poems cough and
metaphors hide
do parables describe or disguise?
if i wrote in rhymes would you read easier?
if i didn't write at all would you breathe easier?
do the words get in the way

umm, the smoothy calypso
and shuffling in, the lady in white, ooo
let her in, the lights lower
open your arms to her
her eyes will open to you
and she'll remake all your mind beauty
throw out your tears to the lady in white
have her, hold her dear close in on you
mating season
bad days are gone

have you discovered yet that this is not a book?

poetry is a stance: accept it and see

if you close your eyes and see the dancing spots, you will
      have created art

should you open them to the world, you will have
      created life

this life/poem jogs along on the tip of your eyelash

your witness